Teeth & Talons

Mood Poems

Katurah McNichols

BookLeaf Publishing

India | USA | UK

Made with ❤ on the BookLeaf Publishing Platform
www.bookleafpub.in
www.bookleafpub.com

Dedication

Dedicated to flowers growing from fingertips, moss, lichen and snails.
Someday.

And to Leah Sawnor, the Vivacious Violet. 8/5/2025.

Preface

I used to write a lot, and then I started painting. I'm trying to do both. To write this book was a challenge I didn't think would be quite so... challenging. I think I write when I'm in a bereft valley, and I paint when I'm in a chaotic peak . So, for my next trick I will learn to interchange those roles.

Acknowledgements

William Oliver
Michael Roger
Lilith Gloria Lee

Lauren, Snickyfritz, Bunsy, Christina Cupcakes, Sarah H, Sarah J, RPW, Rosa

Elliott, Nikki, Nemo, Billy, Jasper, all of the cats everywhere, even the mean ones.

James, Richard, Daniel

Trevor, Spencer, Sharon, Tracy, Tyffanny, Martha, and especially Sioux.

xo
Love, Katurah
2025

1. Seed for Salt

When the snow is heavy and our hands are damp,
pink
and cold,
and we cannot move.
We are stuck, and wheels spin violently.
But, there is no salt.
No rough cut halite gem,
because it may kill the birds.
The friends who leave their tracks upon the deck,
little footprints in the snow,
in the dusting of the early morning.
They bathe in the rain and joke with each other
that all they get are nibbles.
I find a shovel to dig
myself
out
and This is where I fall.
I will get up again,
to shake bird seed on the ice.
Instead of salt.
So I won't kill the birds.

2. Pulling

We will never experience the dimming
of the day together.
When the light is low and the moon
is pulling you like the tide.
Your smooth, rounded corners.
My cornsilk hair, draped in murky
History.
Mine. Yours. It hardly matters.
Dried like paint, thick and grotesque.
Like the weighted skin of mud on canvas.
Warmed by the sun.
Pulling my mind
Pulling my hair
Dragging me down like sand around my
ankles.
Bags to keep from turning over.
While you are building delicate castles,
you breathe air, but I breathe salt.

3. Just to look up sometimes

The wind is with me, and I
am with the wind.
Ever a gale,
a cool breeze.
The crispness of twilight,
the thumbnail moon.
Fingers weaving softly through my memory -
and lips locked in a velvet kiss
from just below the clouds.

4. In March

In March
the earth breathes deeply
inhale and exhaling
with the small cries of spirits, twirling off the warming
lake just east of our house.
The stones, heaved by frost, determined to spoil the
fields.
They are mocked by crows and
fog.
Low and quick
like a geyser's steam,
but it moves with an urgency,
this fog,
these dreams.
Across the fields.
From just behind our house.

5. Ghosts at the Gates

Oh, rejoice in the warmth
by the sunlight in the evening,
a trickery.
For it is just between these realms.
Between this day and the next.
Between this season and the next.
Between this life and whatever lay beyond.
The gates will open briefly,
to let the ghosts catch glimpse of the world they've left
behind.
And the things that never existed and won't exist again,
as soon as they turn the page.

6. Time

Time in, time out
twigs and bones
sticks and stones
broken heart and
fucked up head -
How 'bout we just burn this bed?
Burn it hot and bright as day,
it's not a place I want to lay.
For in it there are many ghosts,
and though I wanted you the most,
it seems I have expired.

7. Big Mama Covid 3x

The porch has bees
And so do I -
Breathy and curt,
fizzing as I cough into a decorative handkerchief,
with little fairies and leaves.
I smother them in my sickness.
Here, my skin crawls with invisible
ticks.
Feasting
Swollen
And, in my fever dreams, you come
as bright as the angels I know do not exist.
Wings like a raptor, featherless, leathery, like an old bag.
A simple syrup of sugar and water,
except all the water is spit and all the sugar -
sweat.

8. When wind knocks down the trees

You dance beyond my curtain
with limbs frenetic
rhythmless.
Whispering. Always whispering.
Singing. Always singing.
Humming and scritching at my window.
Full of pain.
Or Purpose.
And somehow, even in my dreamland, you know which way to turn.
We pass each other gently in the hallway.
Enveloping and hungry,
devouring bones and rustling blankets.
And I am wisped away from here,
carried away on the back of a stray cat.
I cling to the dingy hairs and hope he can avoid the hawks, or worse.
But, waking in the morning light,
I sit and drink my coffee, and
long for the trees.
All the trees are felled.

9. Dewey Decimal

With each warm burst of daylight,
Spring awakens with rocks and stones;
clearing out her mother's pores.
Pouring all her energy into hope and photosynthesis.
The rains appears, and turn it all to mud.
Over and over, waking the earth and preserving fossil
history.
And when the grass turns green,
June will have arrived.
I will be older then, but not the wiser.
A card catalog of decommissioned reference books.
Full of typos. Misunderstood facts.
Disenfranchised agencies.
A lurking paleness.
Entropy.
And a dead fawn at the end of the cul de sac.

10. Ways we understand

I live in blue concrete,
a soft corduroy decay -
dancing through peat and
bleeding red oceans of smoke
to heal this fool of blindness.
Haunting with grace and sound,
ten million blades of soft green grass,
all covered in black ice and shattered glass,
for you to seek and sing about in this harmony.
Understanding flight
the same way you understand hunger
or language
or silence.

11. Vision's not what it used to be

Lights and cables hold me up in the ether.
Like I'm taking flight and
heading for the stars.
Impossible, far away and far too hot.
Or, holding the tail of a kite in a lightning storm.
My canopy is grief and a sack full of teeth.
The best kind. Cavities and all.
My sweet tooth, and
Memories even I cannot recall.
They're dusty and I carry them along,
but never really know them anymore.
Lights flicker,
I know you sense it, too.
As fragile as an Edison bulb,
as lonesome as a child in a hedge maze.
As useless as a fork with a bowl of soup.
As if I were real, and not even invisible anymore.

12. Ode to Miscarriage

I am a tomb
just walking around
all of the fury
without any sound.

Gentle reminders of
things that are lost
with three on the earth
and five in the frost.

13. A sincere lack of concern

I ingest the flames
of this fire; old and greedy
It fills my lungs and overflows with warmth
green lips
blue skin
charred lips
fingertips
pale moon, illuminated in the
solitude of this hammock.
Pockets torn from seams
Doors torn from hinges
Balancing on logs in the pitch
dark
Staring into the moon as it
slowly
Finds its way behind the clouds
Heavy with the ash of you,
and flames put out by tears

14. Smoke Signals

This signal doesn't work.
Hot coffee, birds... sweet seeds that line the walkway,
Morning air, crisp, new, unaware
of the bullshit to come.
I am tortured by memories,
All of them.
And to find out you weren't really there?
That's the worst part.
Am I angry or am I afraid?
Am I sad or am I indifferent?
Because there's nothing else.
No more horizons. No more
pillars out in front of the building.
Like I've said a million times,
There never was, there never will be,
Because I've lost the whole entire
sky.

15. Bound to Earth

I will or
I won't
I guess we'll have to see
Wait
Hurry
jump and crouch
silent reverie
Black and white
or black and blue
1000 speckled stars
teeth
eyes
hands
hairs
I cannot even feel the eggshells beneath my feet

16. For Sydney

October in the veil
tenuous tendrils wrap around each bird's wing
each beak, each feather
as they wisp away
floating like obliging dreams
around my skull
and you have never
been so still
still and silent, breathless
warm and with a bluish tint
your lips and fingertips
Waiting quietly, impatiently,
as they pray to Freya
and you pass from one world to the next
or blackness,
it's impossible to say,
You were a pallette
perfect brush strokes
and inky hands
you were a light
until you figured out how to end the world.

For Sydney Hunt 10/8/2020

17. For DeeDee

Voice of ten thousand laughing songbirds
Deep like the ocean
the blue green sea

I longed to float in your song forever,
your abyss,
your cocoon,
to one day emerge as you did,
A goddess with flaming hair

Eyes that flashed with suddenness
and uncharacteristic calm
A light put out before it's time
And the heaven's rumble: Tazurdee

For Tazurdee Fortunato 09/2020

18. B.C.

It's silent in the theater
the scent of old butter flavoring hangs just above the mildew
and behind me in the projection booth
the heat is rising with the lamps and motors.
But you're so cool,
the clicking of the projector calms you.
The stacks of film reels calm you.
This silent film calms you.
And history consumes you as you file each morsel of knowledge away.
Absorbing.
Private, loyal, uptight, creative.
And then you ran off and joined the circus.
Because it was your dream.
I wish more of us would follow dreams to wherever they may lead us.
But, today your tent comes down.

For Bill Carter, 10/14/2020

19. Burned

I am
little ghostly thoughts,
hushed,
my first companions.
Of sleepy flesh,
and a small star,
this final soft cloud,
as it tastes of sea and sky.

My acrid chaos
An empty church
This garden bird statuette,
Your last confused arrival.

And still, here am I
under the yellow sun
in a wide brimmed hat.

20. To die on this hill

A victim of this hill,
glass pebbles and plaster seagulls,
It's not even real.
The stage is canopied in tree limbs and vines,
green excrement and algae from the bog,
And upon this hill, I rest,
my eyes are glazed with saline,
tears, but from the wind,
this icy wind that hits me in the face
and encourages my mind to dream of lighthouses
and smog.

21. Oh, the places I won't go

The Red Beach in Hormuz, Iran
New Zealand & Tasmania
Space
Down an aisle
In a coffin
Jökulsárlón
Lake Baikal
Back to the start.
All the way to the end.
Machu Picchu
Atacama
Antarctica
and home.